Think Positive on Purpose

Think Positive on Purpose

A practical guide to overcoming negative thinking
and living a fulfilling life

Alyssa L. Akins

ISBN: 978-0-692-17441-8

Copyright © 2018 · Alyssa Akins

Published by InspireU Publishing

Printed in the United States of America

Dedication

This book is dedicated to my daughter Aliciana. You are the inspiration behind this book. Seeing your strength and courage over the years has truly blessed my life and helped develop my faith to another level. My grandson Jasai, you are the light of my life and always keep me laughing. Mom and dad thank you for your love and support and daily inspiration. To all of my family, I love you with all my heart.

Contents

Woman Empowered Affirmation..................ix

Introduction 1

Chapter 1: When life hands you lemons.......5

Chapter 2: Change starts with you............14

Chapter 3: Renew your mind 20

Chapter 4: Take Care of You......................25

Chapter 5: The Healing Process.................32

Chapter 6: Build your legacy......................38

Chapter 7: Trust God..................................48

Chapter 8: Reclaim Your Time...................58

Self-Evaluation 67

Think Positive Highlights 69

Author's Thoughts 70

Woman Empowered Affirmation

I AM the daughter of the Most High God.

I AM unique and refuse to compare myself to others.

I AM highly intelligent and creative.

I AM physically, mentally and emotionally healthy.

My family is blessed and highly favored.

My debts are cancelled; I am financially free.

I AM knowledgeable about saving and investing.

I AM a leader and great role model to my family and community.

Introduction

Victory starts in the mind. Your thoughts can either elevate you or keep you in bondage, making it hard for you to ever find peace and happiness. It can affect whether you go to the next level in your career, relationships, finances, and life in general. There is a battle going on in the mind every day. The enemy (Satan) wants you to believe his lies of defeat, fear, inferiority, inadequacy and anything that is negative and keeps you from believing in yourself and living the best life that God has for you. You must know that every thought that comes across your mind is not your own and you don't have to let it take precedence. Think positive on purpose means that you must force yourself to think positive even though your thoughts may be telling you otherwise. It took me a long time to finally get this. I would struggle with image issues, and the feelings of inadequacy. The lies from the enemy were that I was not beautiful, and I was unworthy of love. I thought that I had to look like the women in the beauty magazines and achieve an unrealistic weight. Truth is if we only know how much those photos are airbrushed! Nobody is that perfect in real life. I am not saying that I have it all together because sometimes I still struggle with my self-image but when those thoughts do occur, I say an affirmation such as, "God, help me to see myself the way you see me." I also will say, "I am beautiful, and I am enough. I embrace and love every curve and everything about me, despite what the world says." I used to believe the lies of the enemy until I learned how to really walk in faith and use the power of God's word to overcome self-defeating thoughts. What thoughts do you struggle with? Do you blame and put yourself down every time something bad happens? What about when things just don't seem to go right in your life as you planned? Your thoughts will tell you that you won't have success and you will never get far in life. You cannot believe those lies. Believe me, it is easy to do, and it is a daily battle you must fight. When we have such self-defeating behavior, it only contributes to the problem and makes things worse. The way you think about yourself and different situations you face can easily affect what you speak as well. Words are powerful, and many people don't realize that they are not getting ahead in life based on not only how they think but how they speak. You're constantly spinning your wheels and facing the same issues repeatedly with no success. But... all hope is not lost! Be confident and know that you can change those negative behaviors and transform them into one that empowers and sets you up for success.

Chapter 1

When life hands you lemons

Do not get weary in well doing,
for in due season you shall reap
a harvest if you faint not.

Galatians 6:9 KJV

When you have a child, who gets seriously ill unexpectedly, you wonder why this is happening, asking yourself whether it is something you did or did not do as a parent. You feel frustrated and angry and begin to question your faith. My daughter went from being a healthy, active and outgoing child to suddenly being extremely ill to the extent that she was told she could no longer do the sports and outdoor activities she loved to do because of a lung infection. She would spend the next several years in and out of the hospital (PICU), seeing multiple specialists and taking a variety of medications. When we were done with the doctors and specialists in our hometown, we were referred to the University of Michigan to see a Pulmonologist. I just knew they would have a clear answer as to what was going on because it was such a highly regarded research and medical institution. I was wrong. They didn't seem to know why my daughter was getting so sick either. Her symptoms mimicked asthma, but normally, asthma is easy to control with medication. Her symptoms often did not budge with treatment, unless she was put on high doses of Prednisone and that was what they tried to avoid. It was such a long and rough road. My daughter was so strong and often handled it better than I thought she would and sometimes better than I. I would break down and cry, sometimes out of frustration. Our lives had changed. I just wanted her to be healthy and able to get back to a normal life. I prayed and prayed, but sometimes God has a different plan than we want. I wanted to fall apart, but I knew I had to be strong for my child. Her strength and will to fight gave me strength but most of all I knew God, and I had been taught to have faith on another level. What I learned about faith was empowering and changed how I dealt with the situation. I learned that death and life are in the power of the tongue and what you think and speak can have a positive or negative impact on your life. I could have let what happened to my daughter break me. I could have lost faith and given up hope, but I knew the God I served. I also knew that this was an attack of the enemy on her health and we were in spiritual warfare. I learned to use the word of God along with my faith to overcome the battles we would face.

I admired my daughter's strength. Even though she missed a lot at school, she was so adamant about doing her homework and keeping her grades up. She was an A/B student and didn't want to jeopardize her grades. She remained as positive as she could and worked hard. There were many long days in the hospital, and often it was just she and I all day. It got lonely at times. We tried to make the best of it by taking walks down the children's wing looking at all the artworks on the windows. We often would go to the kids' lounge and do arts and crafts or play different games. I thank God for Sparrow Hospital and the children's floor staff for working hard to make her and all the kids stay as stress-free as possible. I recall a volunteer who always came to the room daily to bring us a movie list and my daughter would pick multiple movies that she wanted to watch in her room. Though these things may seem small, it meant everything to me to see my daughter have activities she could do that took her mind off of what she was going through, at least for the time being. It is not easy to sit in the hospital for days at a time, so you must find things to do that take your focus off it.

When I think back, God was already showing me that things would work out because we had hope and we didn't allow this situation to define us and control our lives. The blessing is she would go to the hospital for a few days, but she was always able to go back home and to school with her friends and have some normalcy until the next episode. We stayed encouraged as much as we could and kept believing and confessing that God would heal her.

Eventually, by high school, she had outgrown the worst stage of asthma and was able to stop some of her medication which was a blessing. No parent wants to see their child sick let alone being on strong medications. My goal has been not to focus so much on what happened because I do have flashbacks from time to time of that stage of our lives, but I turn those thoughts into something positive. The blessing is that it helped us become stronger Christians and really forced us to rely solely on God. He blessed my daughter to overcome and rise above the sickness. I never stopped putting my trust in God, no matter what the situation looked like. I thought and spoke as if my daughter was already healed. I took my Bible with me to the hospital every time she got admitted, and I read scriptural passages pertaining to healing. I put together a vision-board of empowering words and pictures of my daughter that I looked at and prayed over constantly. I wrote in my journal, talking to God about how I felt and how I wanted Him to heal my daughter. I quoted affirmations about her being healed and living a normal life again. It was freeing, it was empowering, and it was encouraging to know that we were not sitting back passively and letting these attacks on my daughter's health control us and beat us down. Instead, we fought back with the word of God and the power He put on the inside of us to overcome. I was so amazed at my daughter's strength and that she knew to write down and say her affirmations over her health each day. She learned at a young age how to use her faith, and I am so grateful for our church at the time, teaching us the importance of this principle and putting them to work. I was not taught this same principle growing up, but my mother did raise me in church, and I knew about God and how to go to Him in prayer. I saw God's power work in my life as a child, and in my young adult years and so I knew that He answered prayer. So, I learned to trust Him.

Chapter 2

Change starts with you

"Change will not come if we
wait for some other person or
some other time. We are the
ones we've been waiting for. We
are the change that we seek."

-Barack Obama

In order to change some things, some things have to change. As we all know, change is not an easy thing to do. In fact, once we have been programmed to do things a certain way, it becomes the norm for many and can be extremely hard to break. How we grew up can impact how we think if we had family members who always saw the negative side of things. As kids, this becomes embedded in their spirits and eventually becomes a part of their mindsets. Have you ever noticed when you try to find the good in something or are excited about that new car or outfit you got, that one friend has to find something negative about it? People like this find it hard to celebrate you. It has become a part of who they are and is sadly their norm. We don't always consider our thoughts; it is just a normal process we go through daily. The thing is these thoughts shape our lives, what we do, how we act, if we succeed or fail, etc. If you're constantly thinking to yourself, "I will never get a promotion, or I will never get married" then it is more likely than not to be the outcome. Change is tough but not impossible. If you desire to change how you think, you can do that by taking baby steps. It won't happen overnight but be encouraged and just get started.

Change is good

Start by refocusing your thoughts on something more meaningful. Pull out your pen and paper and make a list of 10 positive things you love about yourself. Maybe it is helping others, or maybe it is a talent that you possess. Write it down and repeat it out loud to yourself each day. Making a habit of doing this daily will not only increase your self-esteem and how you feel about yourself, but you will notice how you think and speak will change, and you will attract more positive energy your way.

Watch the company you keep

The people you hang around can play a major role in how you think and speak about yourself and life in general. Do the people around you always have a complaint or never have anything positive to say? Are they full of drama and always down for an argument? Negative people can drain you and bring down your spirits. If you are around them enough, you may start to adopt some of their ways and think and speak destruction which gets you nowhere fast. Surround yourself with positive people who are going somewhere in life and those who will support you and build you up, not tear you down. As the saying goes, misery loves company, and this saying could never be truer. Choose your circle very carefully.

If God be for you, who can be against you? God will work things out in your favor despite what people may do to block your blessings. I can't begin to tell you how many times I have had to minimize my contact with certain people. They think that just because they are not doing anything to get ahead in life that you're not supposed to either. That is far from the truth. Just remember everybody is not meant to be in your circle. If they do not support your vision, then they need to keep it moving.

Stop comparing

Do not get caught up comparing yourself to others just because they seem to have it all. Comparison can cause low self-esteem and make you feel defeated. It can cause you to lose focus and get you off track from what you should be doing. You are a winner! Don't get discouraged over what someone else has accomplished. When you look back over your life, you have plenty accomplishments to be thankful for and you should not take light of that. Everyone has a different path in life, and their timing may be different from yours.

We are all unique in our own way. Embrace your uniqueness and be proud of who you are and what you have achieved thus far. Your season is coming.

Chapter 3

Renew your mind

"And be not conformed to this
world: but be ye transformed by
the renewing of your mind."

Romans 12:2

When it comes to our thoughts, we often accept what comes to mind, not knowing we have the power of the Holy Spirit on the inside of us to cast down destructive thoughts. Allowing our thoughts take control is what often gets people into trouble. They allow their thoughts to lead them in the wrong direction. This can affect relationships, jobs, finances, health, etc. Why? Because it can lead you to do destructive things and make poor decisions that cause long-lasting damage. The good news is you have the power on the inside of you to control your thinking. Imagine how empowering that is, when you make an on-purpose effort to transform your thinking and turn it into one that is uplifting and full of faith.

Believe in yourself

So, you haven't accomplished some of the things you always said you would do, so what...get over it! You can still accomplish your goals and live your dreams if you believe in yourself. There is nothing that a little preparation can't do. George S. Clason from the book, The Richest Man in Babylon wrote, "willpower is the unflinching purpose to carry a task you set for yourself to fulfillment." Use your willpower to encourage yourself and be inspired to move forward today! I always say, "as long as I have breath in my body, I am going to go after every dream I have with everything that is in me. When you think positively about your life and the endless opportunities that are available, it causes you to act differently, move differently and motivates you to go to the next level. You're no longer focused on what the next person is doing because you are prepared with your purpose and a plan. If you put your energy toward your goals, you will start to feel more confident about your future and have a positive outlook on life.

Reading is fundamental

Reading is something that is so powerful, yet so under-rated by many. There is so much that can be learned just by taking 30 minutes a day to sit down and purposely read a book in an area of interest. Believe me, I know it can be hard to focus on reading when we live busy lives and barely have time for anything. One thing, I can say I have discovered is I find solace in reading. It is a form of meditation to me. I go to the bookstore, browse the shelves for books that spark my interest, grab my favorite latte and a comfy chair, and I am good for a few hours. That is my escape from the crazy and busy world we live in. Not only am I learning something new, I am also treating myself to a little R+R.

Attitude Check

You may have heard that your attitude determines your altitude. This saying is very true. There is nothing worse than seeing someone with a poor attitude who can't get along with anyone and always has something bad to say about others. They are never happy and don't find much joy in life. If someone is doing something to better themselves, they find a problem with it because they are not doing anything to elevate themselves. No one wants to be around an attitudinal person. They will suck the life right out of you if you let them. Creativity cannot flow in a negative atmosphere. If this is you, it's imperative that you adjust your attitude if you want to be successful and go to the next level.

Chapter 4

Take Care of You

"Take care of your body. It's the
only place you have to live."

-Jim Rohn

In this fast-paced world, many of us are
often juggling multiple tasks. Between
working, taking care of our kids, attending
school activities, managing things at home,
etc. we forget to stop and take time for
ourselves. If we are not mentally and
physically healthy, we won't be any good to
ourselves or anyone else. A healthy body
equals a healthy mind. I often try to find
activities that are quiet and relaxing such as

going to the bookstore. I can spend hours there. It's not only peaceful but inspiring because there is so much knowledge around you that can be life-changing. Getting involved in the community is another good option. Check out your local Parks and Recreation guide and enroll in a fitness class or a computer class. There are so many options and a great way to stay active and take some time for yourself.

Work that body

Exercise is like a natural medicine. Research has shown that it releases endorphins in the brain that make you feel happy. Often stress and depression can weigh you down, which then leads to self-defeating thoughts. Frequent exercise 3-5 days a week can really make a big difference in how you feel and think. I can tell a big difference in my mindset when I haven't been to the gym in a while. Not only do I notice I lack energy, I also seem to have more negative thoughts. Ladies, you know how we are about our bodies. We are our worst critics, to say the least, judging everybody part and comparing ourselves to other women who may be fitter than we are. When I work out on a consistent basis, I feel more confident, and my thoughts about my image are a lot more positive.

You are what you eat

This saying is so true. If you feed your body junk, then you are going to feel and see the impact of that. Poor eating leads to poor concentration, weight gain, low energy and lack of focus which in turn affects your self-esteem and self-confidence when you don't feel good about yourself. Every day, at work I would crave something sweet. I had to have peanut M+M's almost daily after lunch. I noticed I would start to feel sluggish and lacked energy by mid-day and would doze off at my computer. It finally dawned on me that it was the sugar I was eating that was causing that to happen. You know how they say, sugar gives you a quick boost but then it drops your blood sugar shortly after? Well, it was true. As

I started to decrease my sugar intake I gradually saw a difference in my energy level and focus. I now try not to eat it unless on a special occasion. I try to look at sugar as a rare treat rather than making it a part of my daily diet. Therefore, be cautious of your daily sugar intake, which also includes soda and juice. Try replacing sweets with natural foods, like oranges, watermelon, and grapes. Eating good, wholesome, healthy foods makes you feel so much more energized and focused. You will have a more positive outlook on life because your mind is clear and free from "clutter".

Reality TV isn't so real

Are you caught up in the latest reality television show that's full of the utmost drama? There is nothing real about these reality shows. I refer to them as the new day soap opera. Everyone is literally the same and so predictable. I know because I used to be tied to the television when they would come on. I just couldn't believe some of the low-down things these women would say or do to tear each other down and destroy families and relationships. I just couldn't do it anymore and had to walk away from the nonsense. What about the avid news watchers? They tend to watch nothing but negative news stories every hour on the hour. They don't realize that they are feeding their spirit with overwhelming amounts of bad information. These negative images can have you thinking all sorts of things. My mother is often criticized for watching the news so much; she could not get through the day without watching multiple news shows. I don't see how she does it. Personally, some of the stories stick with me and cause me to have bad thoughts. For example, all the terrorism happening in other countries used to make me worry and wonder if it might start happening here in the United States. I have learned to block negative thoughts and images instantly by replacing them with a happy thought or something funny my grandson said or something I accomplished that I am proud of. You must literally "trick" your mind and purposely refocus on a happier, thought.

Chapter 5

The Healing Process

"I believe that the greatest gift
you can give your family and
the world is a healthy you."

Joyce Meyer

When you're trying to change something
that has been learned over a period of time, it
can be hard to do. Allow yourself to go through
a healing process. It can be healing to spend
time with God. You must go through a healing
process in order to let go of old behaviors and
habits. Spending time with God, your family
and even time with yourself can be healing.
There is nothing like the feeling you get when

you're in the presence of God. He is truly amazing. The love He gives is like no other. There is joy and peace so great that anything negative that tries to come against you has no significance or effect on you. When I have something that weighs heavily on my mind, I sit quietly and talk to God. It really puts my mind at ease.

Spend time with God

This is the most important "nugget" of them all. God wants us to spend time with Him on a daily basis and throughout the day. Yes, our lives get busy, but we should never be too busy to show our love and our appreciation for God and all that He has done for us. I cannot imagine where I would be if it were not for God's grace, love and protection over my family and me. He has delivered us from so many things. I have gone through a lot in my life, but God always delivers me from every situation. His love is amazing!! When those negative and self-defeating thoughts start filling your mind, look up some passages of the scriptures pertaining to your situation and say them aloud. Start to worship God and thank Him for His goodness and mercy and watch the enemy flee.

Do what you love

What is your passion in life? Do you have a favorite hobby that you love to do? What is that one thing that excites you and stirs your creativity? If you are not sure, I challenge you to sit down with your journal and brainstorm what it is that makes you feel good inside and what you really enjoy doing with your free time. When you are doing something that inspires you and/or has meaning, you think differently. It takes your mind off whatever problem it is you're dealing with and allows you to feel free and escape from your worries for a while. It is so important to have something that you enjoy doing. Life will happen, trials and tribulations will come, but If you can find what inspires you and work on developing that thing, you will handle life situations so much easier. See, you can't dwell on a problem and expect it to go away. I find it healing, instead of dwelling on a problem, to work in my journal, or create a new product idea. I am not saying to run from your problems by any means, but while you're going through, you must create positive outlets where you can put that energy toward. Not only that, it can be fun! Give it a try, and you will see the difference.

Give back

Take some time out of your busy schedule to help someone in need. There is always someone out there who may not be as well off and could use a listening ear or a helping hand. There is something about helping others that creates a humble spirit in us. Every year my church takes part in a community giving event during the Christmas holiday. It is heartwarming to see the long lines of church members packing thousands of boxes to deliver to the less fortunate. It is even more touching when we deliver the boxes and see the look on the faces of the parents and children. Just to see their smiles and how thankful they are to receive their food boxes is a feeling that cannot be explained. It is truly what God wants us to do and it a reminder to be thankful in the little things and not take life for granted.

Chapter 6

Build your legacy

"The greatest legacy one can
pass on to one's children and
grandchildren is not money or
other material things
accumulated in one's life, but
rather a legacy of character and
faith."

Billy Graham

Building your legacy means you are
working hard now to create something great
that will benefit not only yourself but your
children and future generations to come.
Many people miss this opportunity because
they can only see what is in front of them.
They don't ever take the time to look toward

the future and plan accordingly. I decided, there is so much more to life than just surviving. If you don't make an on-purpose effort to discover your purpose and walk in it, you may continue to feel stuck in life, your career or lack thereof, etc. You know, I did everything I was supposed to do. I went to college and got a Bachelor's Degree and then went back and got a Master's Degree. I built tons of years of work experience and still none of that has helped me get very far. Am I thankful to have always been employed and never worrying where my next check comes from? Of course! I will never look down on what I have been blessed with, but there comes a point where you must believe in yourself and know your worth. Everyone has gifts and talents they were born with. There is nothing wrong with utilizing those gifts and using them for God's glory by helping others. And you can also turn them into a business that can possibly take you to a higher level in your career. Seek God for wisdom first. Ask Him to give you direction and the confidence to move forward in your gift. Take the lead in creating your own opportunities. Teach your kids the same principle so they know they can have options other than just going to college.

Invest in yourself

Make an investment in self-help books, webinars and other informational products that increase your learning. There is a saying that information changes the seasons of your life. You should always be learning new things and investing in products that increase your wisdom and knowledge. Oftentimes, we get really lax with what we already know and think that is enough. It may be enough if you're satisfied with just getting by, but if you want to go to the next level in your career, finances, health, relationships, etc. you need to spend some money to do so. I have learned so much in the last few years by just reading new books on business and personal development as well as attending conferences and online webinars. This is one of the reasons I have been able to write this book, because through reading and investing in webinars with others who have already been successful at writing a book, not only motivated me to do it but it also taught me what and what not to do. The moral of the story is, do not be afraid to spend money on books, trainings, and products that could be life-changing and take you to another level.

Pursue your passion

What is that one thing that you have always wanted to do and been good at? This may require you to sit down and write out things you used to do when you were younger up through the present. Evaluate school activities you were involved in at one point, volunteer opportunities and hobbies you enjoyed growing up. Determine if there was anything that you consistently enjoyed doing and write it on your list and highlight it, so it stands out. Some of you may not have to go back that far but may already have an idea of what your purpose is, which is great because that means you're halfway there already.

Be Consistent

Whatever it is you choose to do to go to the next level, make sure you are consistent in doing it and putting in the work often. Anyone who is successful will tell you they worked their butt off and put in a lot of blood, sweat, and tears to get to where they are. I have multiple people that I don't know personally, but I get success tips from them on a daily basis. Some of the many people I admire who have an amazing work ethic are Michelle

Obama, Barack Obama, Oprah Winfrey, Steve Harvey, Sean "Diddy" Combs, just to name a few. On Instagram, I am inspired by The Six Figure Chic and The Glam University. They are all very successful, influential and have worked extremely hard to get to where they are today. They are not afraid to share advice and their top secrets with their audience on how to achieve success. I am also inspired by Steve Harvey. He has been through a lot and gives some of the best advice on life, business and believing in your dreams. One of my favorite quotes by him is "If you are persistent you will get it. If you are consistent you will keep it."

Remove Distractions

Distractions will make or break your success. So many things will come along to throw you off track and keep you from focusing on the task at hand. You have to make a choice as to what is most important to you. You won't get very far if you let every distraction take you away from what you're supposed to be doing. I have to check myself on this often. There is always going to be something to be done around the house, people calling or texting, etc. Or maybe your favorite television show is coming on right as you're getting ready to put some time in on your project. This is bound to happen to all of us, and sometimes you can't always control it, but we can control how we respond to it. One of our biggest distractions is our cell phones. We always have to have our phone right next to us or at least where we can see it. If your phone is lighting up every five minutes due to people texting you or your constantly getting notifications from social media, then you must turn the phone off or put it in another room while you work. I can't begin to tell you what a major distraction my phone has been, and I am not going to lie, it's right next to me as I type this, but I am working on it and getting better every day...so I think! There are plenty of times I have trained myself to put it out of my sight which truly helps me focus so much better and get more done. The point is to get in a quiet place where you can think and be creative.

Other distractions outside of electronics could be coming from you. If you're a busy person and have different things going on in your life, you could have a racing mind. This can make it hard to get anything done because you may constantly be thinking about work, your kid's school activities, bills and the other many responsibilities you must take care of. The best thing to do if you have a racing mind is to get in a few minutes of light physical activity such as dancing or running in place. Some people like to sit in a quiet place and meditate in order to calm their mind. I personally think that is a great way to ease a busy mind but do what works best for you.

Chapter 7

Trust God

Trust in the Lord with all your
heart and do not lean on your
own understanding

Proverbs 3:5

Learn to trust God on your journey to overcoming self-defeating behaviors. It took years to learn the behavior, so it will take some time for you to change it. Without trust in God, you cannot expect to get very far in life. If we truly want to change and want God to help us, we must be willing to put all our trust in Him. God wants to have a deeper connection with us. He is longing to get more of your time. It's so important to set aside time to purposely talk to God and share your thoughts and desires with Him. He cares about the things you care about and wants you to put your trust in Him no matter what the situation looks like. Often, when you go through something challenging it feels comfortable to speak or think in a negative manner. It's easy to do because that's what you're going through at the time. The good news is we don't have to deal with challenges by ourselves. God said that He would fight our battles for us. How amazing is that, to know we can depend on His power and strength and not on our own?

Reality vs. Faith

You must learn to trust God even when your situation looks bad. When the doctor says, there is nothing else they can do; you must let your faith take over and trust that God is going to work things out in your favor. You can trust God in any situation that you may be facing. When I have bills that are overdue, and I don't have enough money to cover them, I touch each bill and pray over them, asking God for help. I start to thank Him as if the bills are already paid in full. James 2:14-26 says, Faith without works is dead. Therefore, you must not only ask God for His help, but you also have to believe and act as if you know He is going to follow through.

Where it gets tough is the waiting part. God doesn't do things in our timing and when we want Him to. He does things in His own timing. Patience is truly a virtue, and it is not an easy thing to do. When you need something to happen right now, it is very difficult to have to wait for things to work out. Sometimes it is a matter of waiting, but you also have to do the things that are in your power to change the situation as well. For instance, when my daughter was sick, we started to research alternative medicine and educated ourselves on natural supplements pertaining to her situation along with eating certain types of foods that could heal the body. We saw a great naturopathic doctor in Ann Arbor, MI. His name is Dr. John Sandweiss, and his extensive knowledge and experience with the use of Asian medicine helped my daughter tremendously. We are not supposed to sit back passively and wait for God to do everything, He wants us to use our faith and take the initiative as well. When we activate our faith, God goes to work on our behalf. Therefore, there is nothing wrong with taking some faith steps on our own. God still has the final say this is true, but He doesn't mind us utilizing our faith and taking some action which shows our trust in Him.

Faith over Fear

Faith and fear cannot co-exist. You cannot say that you have faith but walk in fear. I am not saying that it is always easy because I struggle with it at times myself. Fear is a lie from the enemy. You will begin to think the most negative thoughts about something before it even happens and who's to say that it will happen just because you think it. Every thought is not your own. The enemy wants to confuse you and keep you in a fearful and worried state of mind. Why? Because you cannot trust God when you're in this state of mind. You lose hope and feel defeated, and this allows the enemy to come in and take over. You will start to feel as if your situation will never get better. You don't see a way out, and you start to feel hopeless and lose touch with God. Further away from Him you get day by day, and your situation looks even worse to you because you lost your faith. Depression and so many other things can start to form in that space. This is not the route you want to go, and you must fight with all your might to keep your faith and not let fear settle in.

Prayer and Affirmation

Some may think this sounds cliché, but there is power in prayer and saying affirmations. It can really be life-changing because it empowers you and makes you feel like you have some control over your problems and life in general. These are two of the spiritual tools that God has given us to use to cast down the obstacles in our path. Praying is your personal time with God, to talk to Him about anything that is on your mind. It is the direct connect to the kingdom. The dictionary defines prayer as a solemn request for help or expression of thanks addressed to God or an object of worship. Prayer is powerful because it opens the door to our blessings. There are things we just do not have the power to do so we rely on God's power to do them. God can work miracles. He can bless us in ways we could never imagine. If it is in His will, then He can make it happen.

An affirmation is defined as the action or process of affirming something or being affirmed. Therefore, whatever you believe to be true for yourself you can affirm it by speaking it or writing it in your journal. I choose to do both. I have a list of affirmations that I like to say most days. Usually morning is a good time to do it because it sets the pace for my day and fills me with positive energy.

When you feel positive, that energy will rub off on those around you and if it doesn't then it will at least keep the negative people away from you. An affirmation can be something you state about your finances, career, family, health, etc. One of my favorite affirmations that I have been saying lately is, money flows to me in abundance...all my debts are canceled...I am financially free! That makes me excited as I type this. I say this often, and I truly believe it will happen sooner than later. I don't believe that it is God's will for me to live paycheck to paycheck and barely make ends meet. I do not believe that He would want me to be stressed out about bills and worrying how I am going to cover them from month to month. I use the word of God along with my faith to state my affirmations. It is so empowering because the more you say it, the more you believe it to be true. Even though you might not see it yet, you have a strong sense that it will come to pass because you know it's in the scripture. As a matter of fact, I have provided a list of affirmations in the first few pages of my book for your own personal use. State the ones that apply to you or write out your own list of affirmations and post them on your bedroom mirror and recite them each morning when you get up.

Chapter 8

Reclaim Your Time

"Your time is precious and
something that you can never
get back, so use your time
wisely."

-Alyssa Akins

If you don't set aside time to work on your goals they may never manifest. Time is a very precious commodity that is often wasted in so many ways. How many times were you supposed to work on that new project, business or hobby but you got caught up in your favorite television show, or browsing the internet? It seems we can find everything else to do but make time for the things that really matter. If we're not careful, years will have passed us by, and we will still be trying to start that same old project. Just remember there are many people who are living out their dreams and doing what they have always wanted to do. They had to start somewhere. It didn't just happen overnight. What's important is that we just get started and even if we do a little at a time just be consistent. It's time to start making moves if you want to see change.

Refocus and Recharge

You may have to start fresh from time to time and develop a new strategy in order to get where you're going. It's normal to get off track sometimes because there is so many other things that we may be doing. In today's fast-paced society, people are so consumed with technology and often are wrapped up in thoughtless time stealers such as our cell phones and iPad. Think about it, how many hours a day do you spend on average browsing social media sites? I know it is a lot for me and I beat myself up for it every time because I know I could have used that time doing something so much more productive. It is so easy to get caught up in what others are posting and looking at pictures, etc. Before you know it, you have spent two or more hours on your phone.

Reclaim your time by setting a schedule for the day and deciding when you will do certain activities. For instance, you can set aside a maximum of an hour for browsing the internet in the evening but after you have spent time on your important tasks first. In fact, research shows that you should end all use of technology at least two hours before bedtime or else it could interfere with your sleeping pattern. It is important to not waste your time on mindless activities if you want to get anything accomplished. I do believe there is enough time in the day if you purposely schedule it in. Focus your time and energy on things that matter and watch your goals start to manifest.

Set Clear Goals

It is important to set clear goals if you are going to go the next level in your career, finances, health or whatever area you decide to focus on. It is one thing to say you want to do something, but it is a lot more effective if you write your goals down so that you can see them in front of you. Decide what it is you really want to accomplish and determine in order of importance what you will work on first. This may seem overwhelming in the beginning, but if you break each goal down into small parts and focus on one at a time, it won't seem like such a big task. Everything does not have to be done at once; it can be done over a specific amount of time that you decide but do try to put a completion date on it. This will motivate you to get it done rather than dragging your feet on it and possibly never completing it.

Organizing your goals in an orderly fashion is a great motivator. Select a business notebook or an inspirational notebook with an empowering quote that you can record all the details of your progress in. I feel as if I am more motivated to get things done if I am organized. Keep your notebook in the same area each time you're done with it, so you can always easily get to it when you need to.

See your vision come to life

After you have written out your desired goals, the next step is to create a vision board where you can see your dreams and goals in front of you in a picture form. A vision board is a collage of images, pictures, and affirmations of your dreams, goals, and things that make you feel good about yourself. It can include photos of you're a home you see yourself buying one day, a business you want to start, the wedding of your dreams, positive words and quotes and a trip you have always dreamed of taking, the list goes on and on. It is technically your dream board. It is such an empowering tool because it motivates you and reminds you that you must work hard if you want to achieve what you see in the pictures.

This is a tool that many corporations use today. They understand the power of a vision-board because it works like a blueprint for the company. The company may use it to forecast future sales and determine what direction they want to take the company in, develop new products, etc. The point is, if companies can use them to be successful, then that says a lot about the power they possess and how beneficial they can be to other goal-getters.

The way you think can determine the direction you go in life. I hope that you will apply the steps discussed in this book to your everyday life. I want to see you win and live your best life possible. When negative thoughts start to overwhelm you and have you speaking and or acting in a destructive way, remember to take those thoughts and turn them into something more productive and beneficial to your life. It's not always the easiest thing to do but with constant practice; it can be done. You will start to see so much favor come your way and prayers being answered. I challenge you to get started right away. Be sure you keep a journal to track your day and how you manage your thoughts as well as your mouth which is just as important. Love yourself, embrace your differences, acknowledge your accomplishments and no matter what happens on your journey, keep looking forward and think positive on purpose!

Self-Evaluation

1. What did you take away from this book?

2. What negative thoughts have you in bondage and keep you from getting ahead?

3. How do you normally handle those thoughts?

4. What would you say are some of the factors that contribute to your negative thoughts? List your top 3.

5. List here how you can turn negative thoughts into a positive affirmation.

6. Do you believe in the power of positive thinking and how it can impact your life?

Think Positive Highlights

- Your thoughts can either elevate you or keep you in bondage.

- Every thought is not your own.

- Refocus your thoughts on things that are important to you.

- Surround yourself with positive people who are going somewhere in life.

- Don't get discouraged over what someone else has accomplished.

- Replace negative thoughts with something positive.

- You must learn to trust God even when your situation looks bad.

Author's Thoughts

It is my hope that you will discover your God-given power on the inside of you and use it to overcome the challenges life throws at you. Your situation does not have to define you, but it will if you let it. Combine the power of your thoughts with your faith to think the opposite of what you're going through and instead, imagine a positive outlook. Use adversity as a tool that builds you up and makes you stronger. You, my friend, are a child of God...act like one!

www.ingramcontent.com/pod-product-compliance
Lightning Source LLC
Chambersburg PA
CBHW050600280326
41933CB00011B/1920